CW00688499

The 10 Rules o

10
THE
RULES OF SUCCESS

Mridula Agarwal

Rupa & Co

Typeset in 12 pts. Souvenir by
Nikita Overseas Pvt. Ltd.
1410 Chiranjiv Tower
43 Nehru Place
New Delhi 110 019

Printed in India by
Gopsons Papers Ltd.
A-14 Sector 60
Noida 201 301

Contents

Introduction

S uccess is something that we all aspire for. We cannot feel genuinely happy for long if we feel like a failure within. The most encouraging reality about success is that it is attainable by all, irrespective of who we are, what we are or where we are. Success also has a different meaning for each one of us.

Success, being a personal realisation, should logically be achievable by all, but, we know that this is not really so. Most of us are unable to accomplish what we really want to or what we work for. When we struggle for success and do not get it we become frustrated and this leads us further from our goal. This is what has inspired me to study and write about this complex subject.

Achieving success is your right and you can realise it with ease provided you go about it the right way. You just have to know the rules and apply them in your life. There is no reason why you cannot conquer the heights of your aspirations. There always is, and will be, room at the top; you just have to know your way up.

The ten rules of success that you will find in this book are the universal rules of attaining meaningful success.

They are simple to understand and easy to follow. You will discover not only what to do and how to do it, but, you will also know how these various principles work and what they do. You will have a clearer perception of your life and circumstances and will know what it is that you need to do differently.

Start now and realise your full potential. Always know that you are smarter than you think you are and have the right to be successful, no matter what. You just have to assimilate these rules with determination and let them do wonders for you.

Good luck. The crown of glory is waiting for you.

Rule
One

Success Has A Different Meaning For All

Achieve your goal and wear the crown.

Our right to Success

Work for it and get it

When God made hands
He gave us the ability to work.

Once there was a famous guru. He had two disciples. When their education was complete, and they were ready to leave, the guru called one of them and asked,

'Now that your education is complete and it is time for you to leave and find your own place in the world, what plans do you have for your future?'

The disciple said, 'When I go into the world I will look for success and prosperity.'

The guru gave him a bag full of gold coins, blessed him, and allowed him to leave.

Now the guru called the second disciple and put the same question to him.

He replied, 'I will go into the world and achieve success and be prosperous.'

The guru gave him one silver coin, blessed him, and let him go.

There was a passerby resting a few yards away. After both the disciples had left he went up to the guru and asked him why he gave a bag full of gold coins to the man who was going to look for success and prosperity for himself, while he gave only one silver coin to the man who wanted to achieve success on his own.

The guru smiled and replied, 'the man who is going to look for success and prosperity is unlikely to find it as he will be dependent on external forces for his accomplishments. He will need this bag of gold; it will not last long with him. The second man,' he said, 'is set to achieve success on his own, he will get it. He will also be at peace with himself. He does not need gold from me; he will earn enough for himself. I gave him one silver coin which is what he needs for his bus journey to his destination'.

The passerby thanked the guru and left an enlightened man.

Success is achieving one's chosen goals. The goals that one aspires for and has worked for, whatever they may be. It is the favourable outcome of our endeavour, it is the realisation of what we hold dear to our heart. Success is relative in nature and does not and cannot have any one meaning for all. It is an individual experience and is measured and felt differently by each one of us. It is socially objective but personally subjective. It is objective in areas where it is judged collectively, i.e. examinations and competitions; it is subjective in areas of personal aspirations and goals and in our individual sense of fulfilment. It is evaluated by others but felt by the individual. Society measures it mostly in terms of power, money, and fame, but we have our own standards, and this is what makes it a unique experience.

Success also has a different meaning for each one of us. For a politician it may be attainment of power, for an entrepreneur, amassing wealth; for an artist, achieving fame; for a family man, raising responsible kids; for an athlete, breaking previous records; for a scientist, the invention or discovery of something new; and for yet another man, it may be the realisation that all this is useless and he may feel fulfilled leading a simple life.

Cherie Carter-Scott, in her book, *If Success Is a Game, These Are the Rules*, says, *For me, having a profound impact on one person's life means that my life was not lived in vain. Each time I lead a workshop and see the spark ignite in one participant's eye, I feel as if I have succeeded. Seeing people change their behavior, fulfilling their dreams, ending a cycle of self-sabotage, beginning to earnestly love themselves is what brings me a deep sense of fulfilment.*

Success, being relative, also has a different scale of measure for all of us. A man with a lot of money who is the envy of all may not always be successful in the eyes of his society or to himself. A man worth a hundred million, who inherited a thousand million, is a big failure in the eyes of everyone, he is a great comedown. Had he added another ten million to his assets, it would still be no big deal. But for a self made man, making ten million would be a huge success. A counter clerk is successful when he becomes the shift-in-charge, but a store manager has to become the General Manager to be so.

Whatever personal definition of success we may have, one thing is certain, each one of us has the right to be successful, and success is attainable to one and all.

Success in life depends not so much on opportunity and talent as on planning and execution, and least of all on luck. Luck may, at times, appear to play an important role, but luck is known to knock on the door of the deserving, others do not hear the knock. The one basic law that governs all success is that rewards in life are in direct proportion to our effort, and that we, and only we, can make it happen.

As the Swedish saying goes, *when luck offers a finger, we must take the whole hand.* The Greeks say, *the wise carries his fortune with him.* And Bacon has said, *A wise man will make more opportunities than he can find.*

Success requires its share of hard work, dedication and perseverance. There are no short cuts and it can also not be wished. The politician will have to work for the people to be able to lead them for long; the entrepreneur will have to work on his project to harvest its rewards; the artist will have to practise his art with dedication for a good performance; the family man will have to give time to his kids and teach them values; the athlete will have to develop his stamina and train for his sport to be able to break all records; the scientist will have to acquire knowledge to make his contribution to the world of science; and the simpleton will have to have a simple heart and make sure it is not a refuge from hard work, or a defence against failure. Simplicity can be fulfilling only as a choice.

Albert Einstein once said, *Possessions, outward success, publicity, luxury – to me these have always been contemptible. I believe that a simple and unassuming manner of life is best for everyone, best both for body and mind.*

Our individual goals and the road to them may be different but we have one thing in common, we have to work towards our goals, and we have to work ourselves. No one else can do it for us. We have to climb our own steps, and there is always room at the top. Getting pulled up is like the swing of a pendulum; you always keep coming down.

Another characteristic of success is that success is a journey, not a destination, you have to move ahead. If you stay put, you go down, either by your own weight, or will be left behind. In attaining meaningful success one step leads to the next and we climb one step at a time. When our son got admission to the top medical school in the country we were very happy, we thought he had made it, he had arrived. But very soon we realised that this was not so. Before we knew it, it was time for him to work for the next stage, i.e. specialisation, and then super specialisation, then placement of his dreams, and the journey is not yet over. Now he is working to gain heights, and heights have no ceilings. Nowhere along the line could he have stopped and felt fulfilled for long, had he not moved on to the next step.

Climbing the ladder of success is like climbing a mountain. Every peak is a destination, and you climb one peak at a time. Reaching every destination is a challenge well met, and the splendour of it enthralls you on arrival. You find a new landscape stretched out in front of you bestowing its beauty on you, and as you stand there feasting your eyes on it you slowly realise there is another peak out there, shining in the horizon, challenging you. If you do not move on to it, some one else will. This in no way means that life is a race and you have to run all the time. Instead, it is a journey that keeps you going. This is what gives meaning to life and the thrill to be alive. The only thing we must guard against is not to get trapped in a race and tire ourselves. There is a subtle difference between getting trapped in a rat race and marching the road to success. We shall talk about it later in this book.

1. Success is a relative term; it has a different meaning for all, and, as such, is measured and felt differently by all of us.
2. Success depends on planning and its execution, not luck. If you wait for luck to shine, it never will, you have to go and get it.
3. Success requires its share of hard work and dedication; there are no short cuts, and it can also not be wished.

Rule
Two

Have Faith in Yourself

The best platform to stand on are your own two feet.

Believe You Can Succeed

Conquer Your Fears

The best hands to work with
Are your own two hands.

They can conquer who believe they can.—Dryden

All successful people have one thing in common— they have faith in themselves. No progress can be made without the knowledge of the possibility to succeed. The effort we put in our work is in direct proportion to our confidence in our capacity to accomplish.

Who can have more faith in us but we ourselves? All of us have experienced times when we knew in advance that we would succeed and we did, or vice versa, when we were apprehensive and did not. What you tell yourself and what you believe in is what you will ultimately be able to achieve. An athlete who is afraid of falling mid-way cannot take a winning jump; a singer who is not confident of her talent cannot give a breath-taking performance; a scientist who has no confidence in his knowledge cannot invent; a writer with no confidence in his writing cannot write. Confidence is the key to all success.

> David J. Schwartz, in his famous book, *The Magic of Thinking Big,* says, *Belief in success is one basic, absolutely essential ingredient in successful people. Believe, really believe, you can succeed and you will.*

When we believe we can succeed our entire self helps us find ways of doing it. We automatically observe and learn from other successful people around us, and we also find the stamina to do what needs to be done. We do not get discouraged by setbacks, but learn from them instead. Our confidence in our success brings us success.

> *Confidence imparts a wondrous inspiration to its possessor.—It bears him on in security, either to meet no danger, or to find matter of glorious trial.*   —Milton

The only problem with confidence is that it needs a solid base. We cannot fool ourselves into feeling confident; we have to be sure of our worth. And for this we have to be really worthy of what we want to achieve, we have to have the required talent and skill needed for the job. And this needs hard work.

The main obstacle in our working hard towards our goals is our lack of faith in ourselves and in our capacity to excel. When we are not sure of our capacity and talent we are afraid that if we work hard and do not achieve what we want to it will be evidence of our not being as capable as we would like to believe. This is exactly why children who are overpraised by their parents or teachers never work hard. Consider a situation when a mother of an average student says, 'my child is very bright, he just does not work hard', What will this child do? He wants to hold on to the 'bright child' label given to him by his mother without his being really worthy of it. He knows what his mother is saying may not really be true. His average achievements to date are no secret to him and now he is afraid that if he works hard he runs the risk of exposing his true worth to his mother, and he is smart enough not to let that happen. He simply refuses to work hard.

We will run a race only when we are confident of our capacity to run. The capacity to run cannot be wished, it has to be built with regular training and exercise and the true extent of our training is never hidden from us. Till we have equipped ourselves with the required talent we will not want to make an effort at the risk of failing. We will prefer not to make that effort at all. Even if we are forced into it our effort will be half-hearted and we are likely to quit mid-way.

I once had this average student in my class; he never took his work seriously and was always late with his assignments. He enjoyed disturbing the class during studies. He would cut jokes and make fun of the top students; he would call them 'bookworms' and try to bully them. One day I asked him what he would do if he knew he could top in the class? The question took him by surprise. At first he was not prepared to contemplate on the possibility of being able to top, he thought it was a big joke, that I was making fun of him (see how he was judging my intentions through his own eyes) but when he understood the seriousness of my question he contemplated on it and said, 'work hard, what else?'

All strength and force of man comes from his faith in things unseen. He who believes is strong; he who doubts is weak. Strong convictions precede great action.
—J. F. Clarke.

To be able to work hard you have to have the confidence that you will succeed in what you are doing and for that you have to have faith in yourself. When your inner self tells you, 'you won't be successful', you believe it; when you tell yourself, 'I can't do it', you really cannot do it. Nobody has better access to your ears than your own voice. Your body and mind will know what you know and they won't co-operate. On the other hand if you say to your self 'I can', you will find that you can. The moment you tell yourself that you can achieve your goal your brain will know it and start functioning on how to make it possible. We are our own masters and nothing dominates our mind more than our own thoughts. When we believe we can, and when we believe we can't we are right both ways. We make it so.

Man could learn to fly only when he had faith in himself and his ability in making it possible. He did not stand on a rooftop wishing for the winds to take him up, instead he studied the dynamics of flying before he became confident enough to make his first attempt. Imagine how daring it was of him to even visualise such a seemingly impossible dream, let alone make an attempt. Small failures on the way did not stop him, he knew he would win and he did. Envisage where this world would be if we did not have individuals with such extraordinary faith in themselves, and imagine where it will be if we have more of this kind.

What I admire in Columbus is not his having discovered a world, but his having gone in search for it on the faith of an opinion.

—Turgot

No big venture can be undertaken without faith. Nothing can be truer than the saying, 'your attitude determines your altitude', wherever you place yourself you will reach, your sight will determine your height. Your attitude towards your ability is determined by your past experiences coupled with your positive or negative orientation towards yourself. What you think you can achieve you will be able to achieve, and what you think you deserve, you will get.

I would not be writing this book had I not worked hard on it and was not sure of its success. And you would not be reading it if you were not sure of your ability to benefit from what you read, or did not have the desire to learn. This speaks of your confidence in you and what you do.

Confident people also have the advantage of being better heard and better understood. People tend to listen more to them. Watch people when they walk into an office or a store, the confident looking man will get the best attention. Your confidence will speak for itself without saying. Have we not felt our posture change and our voice ring clearer when we are feeling confident? Can't we all know something about the confidence level of a stranger when he walks into a room?

The world belongs to the man who has faith in himself. When you believe you can do something, how-to-do-it follows. How else could man soar into the skies, let alone land on the moon. All progress in this world was made possible because someone out there had faith in himself; he knew he could do it.

When my friend wanted to start her own jewellery business with a modest capital and no experience, everyone, including her family and friends, discouraged her form doing it. Even her husband thought she would not succeed. When she persisted it was widely believed that she would soon tire and quit, after all she had no experience and not enough money. Besides, it was also difficult for a new entrepreneur to break into the cartel, she was told.

But her confidence in herself combined with her determination, dedication, and hard work has paid dividends. She did have a few setbacks in the beginning, but she used them to learn more about her trade and gained experience from them. Now, after ten years, she has a flourishing business and her husband also lends her a helping hand whenever he can. Her turnover this year was more than three million.

*In actual life every great enterprise begins
with and takes first forward step in faith.*
                                        —Schlegel.

People who attain heights are no different from the
ordinary people around us. The only difference is that the
average man regards himself a mediocre. He has been
conditioned to believe that the top slot is not for him and
he will not be able to achieve anything significant in life.
He is afraid of dreaming big. 'Growth is like a pyramid'
he has been told, with no room at the top. And he believes
it. He makes no attempt to climb the ladder of success,
he is afraid to set his sight high. 'There is no room at the
top' rings clear in his mind and he is afraid of making an
attempt to move up, he is afraid of slipping down the
'*pyramid*' of success. He does not look at the skies with
no limits and no space crunch. Those few who dare to
look at the stars, rise.

Our readiness to think mediocre is also a major obstacle
on our road to success. We are repeatedly told, 'be practical,
do not aim too high' and we fall in line. Our keenness
to listen to these negative thoughts is influenced partially
by our mediocre conditioning and partially because we
are afraid of hard work. Hard work requires confidence
and when we do not work hard we have an easy excuse
for our failures.

Another big enemy of faith is fear. It manifests itself in many ways and erodes our confidence in ourselves. Fear can be of many kinds; fear of failure in an examination, fear of meeting people, fear of not being heard, fear of not being able to make a good impression, fear of not being able to speak up for ourselves, fear of being jilted in romance, fear of making a bad investment, fear of not being able to raise responsible kids, and the list can go on. Whatever kind of fear we may have, one thing is certain, all fear is real and it cannot be wished away. We can also not fool ourselves into believing we are not afraid and banish fear. Not acknowledging our fears will not help; it will only implant them deeper.

The one way to conquer fear is to work on it. If we are afraid of failing in an examination nothing can make us feel confident than to study more; if we are afraid of people, nothing will help us till we re-orient our thinking, either on our own, or take help, if we feel the need; If we are afraid of being jilted in romance, nothing will help us till we give it a try with a positive attitude; if we are afraid of making a bad investment we should study the investment market better before we decide to invest. Knowledge of what we are doing and how to do it helps overcome fear and this is always possible. If we do not address our fears at their roots they will keep resurfacing from time to time till we work on them and overcome them. A difficult situation paralyses us into inaction till we take action.

> According to Schwartz, *When we face tough problems, we stay mired in the mud until we take action. Hope is a start. But hope needs action to win victories.*

When we do not know how to tackle a situation we tend to procrastinate, but when we force ourselves to confront it we find that our fear vanishes and we are able to handle the difficult situation better. This is what normally happens when a parachute jumper takes his first jump. Till he is in the aircraft waiting to jump he is afraid, but once he jumps, either on his own or is made to, he becomes confident and is able to open his parachute well in time to land without killing himself. With each successive jump he becomes more and more confident and apt. If he is allowed to stand and wait for his fear to disappear before he leaves the plane he will become more fearful with every passing minute, and taking the jump will become increasingly difficult, if not impossible.

Lack of confidence can also be the outcome of a negative memory bank. Man is essentially the sumtotal of his past, what he has experienced and stored in his memory is what is relevant to him and will influence his future behaviour. Our experience is our personal interpretation of events that have taken place in our lives, what we have felt and experienced according to our own interpretations is the only truth for us irrespective of what it really was.

Your mind knows what you feed it. If you tell yourself negative thoughts you will get discouraged from taking any challenge. If you say to yourself 'you are not good at anything, remember the last time you tried and failed', 'you do not have the right knowledge to handle this work', 'don't make a fool of yourself, remember how people made fun of you last time when you attempted it and were unsuccessful', you are very likely to get disheartened and quit. On the other hand if you tell yourself positive things like, 'you sure can do it, remember how you were successful in your earlier work', 'you are better experienced to handle it now', 'remember how you were appreciated when you attempted your previous problem', 'even if you are not successful at first, attempting it will make you wiser', you are likely to attempt and succeed.

Self-trust is the essence of heroism.
—Emerson.

All of us encounter pleasant and unpleasant, encouraging and discouraging, good and bad, positive and negative situations in life every day. It is the successful who remember the pleasant and encouraging ones while the unsuccessful will mostly remember the unpleasant and the negative ones. Nothing can erode our confidence in ourselves more than a store of negative experiences in our mind, the memory of our failures and disappointments, frustrations and setbacks. On the other hand a positive thought can boost us up any time. When we think of all the good things that have happened to us we automatically feel encouraged and confident.

Try this for yourself and see how easy it is, just close your eyes for a few seconds, relax, and smile (even if you do not feel like smiling force yourself to do it) now think of an experience when you were successful and happy and felt encouraged. Don't you feel a little more confident and happy than what you were a moment ago?

Another common problem with our self-confidence is that most of us are vulnerable to the opinions of other people around us. When they tell us that a task is difficult for us we tend to believe them, we get discouraged and run the risk of quitting. Successful people, on the other hand, will not be discouraged by the negative opinions of others, they will question their judgement and ask, 'why not', then ponder on the reasons if there are any, learn from them if required, and move ahead. A successful person knows that there is nothing that someone else can do and he cannot. He has faith in himself and this is all that is important to him. Always remember, if you limit yourself in any way it is of your own choosing.

> Cherie Carter-Scott says, *if you trust yourself, you naturally put all your energy behind your choice. When you stand behind your choices, your chances for success are multiplied.*

Look at all the successful people around you; see how they have faith in themselves, and how they sustain it in crisis. See how they treat setbacks as stepping-stones to success and learn from them on the way. See how they shun all negative thoughts about themselves and others too. If you look at the faults of others, for reasons other than the intention of learning from them, you run the risk of having them rub on to you too. See how successful people disregard unfavourable opinion of others where they know it is not relevant, or learn from it where they feel it is wise to do so. Also see how they ignore the faults of others where they do not concern them. And see how they march ahead on their way to success.

Faith is something that all of us can acquire with a little effort and right thinking. It is the magic word that has done wonders in this world. It can do the same for you too. There is no reason why you cannot have faith in yourself, always know that you are your own master and are inferior to none unless you make it so. Developing faith in yourself is not as difficult as it may sometimes appear to be. Keep these tips in mind and have them do wonders for you.

1. Always remember that you are better than what you think you are. Failures are the stepping-stones to success for the wise; your belief in yourself is all that is important. Picture your success in your mind's eye, plan and proceed.
2. Never be afraid of hard work .No one reaches the top without climbing the steps.
3. Don't let fear of any kind stop you. Fear is not to be afraid of; it is to be worked at.
4. Clear your mind of all negative thought and concentrate on your achievements. Make a positive memory account. Do not allow any negative thought either about yourself or other people crowd your mind. Negative thoughts do not produce positive results.
5. Don't be afraid of dreaming big. Big dreams bring big results. You can't plan a small house and build a palace.

6. Negative opinions of other people are to be ignored, we know more about ourselves than they do.
7. Look at the successful people around you; see how they work and manage themselves and their affairs; how they plan in advance; how they overcome their obstacles.
8. Always know if others can do it you can do it too.

Rule
Three

Change. Learn and Improve.

If you do not change you will become obsolete.

You can Change if YOU Choose to Change

Grow with the time

If you do not change,
Life will change you,
But not on your terms.

C hange is the essence of life, don't be afraid of it. I remember when I was in the first grade in school we were taught the difference between the living and the non-living things. We were told that living things changed with time while the non-living stayed as they were. Change being the essence of life, some change is inevitable in all and is taking place every day; it is a universal and unavoidable phenomenon. The basic question here is not whether we are changing or not but are we changing for the better or for worse? Are we changing to improve and grow or to degenerate and perish? Are we changing the way we want to change or are we being led into it by time and circumstances?

Bacon has said, *he that will not apply new remedies must expect new evils.*

No progress can take place without change. You can't put your knowledge and experience to use without learning from it and all learning results in change. Learning that does not lead to change is like a book on the shelf, waiting to be read.

Though we all know that some change is inevitable and is universal to all, we come across people who are resistant to change. They may, at times, take pride in saying, 'I won't change, come what may' and they try their level best not to let it happen. This resistance to change is either the outcome of a faulty perception of life, or some inner conflict or insecurity, or both, that the person may be suffering from. Resistance to change can lead to a very rigid attitude to life, and rigidity stalls all growth. Man is successful only because of his superior intelligence which makes it possible for him to adapt to and control his environment according to his needs, and this he does by either changing himself or his environment to suit those needs. No other species has this ability to the extent that man has, and this is what makes him superior to all.

Change is growth and growth is never static, it is a continuous and multidimensional process. It can be positive or negative, you either go up or come down, but you never stay at the same place for long. Change is relevant in all areas of human development and learning. In this book we are dealing with positive change; change that will lead us to the kind of growth we desire for and are looking forward to; change that will inspire us and stay with us for ever; change that will bring peace of mind and make us happy.

> *Today is not yesterday.—We ourselves change.—How then, can our works and thoughts, if they are always to be the fittest, continue always the same?* —Carlyle

Psychologists say, and with enough evidence and proof, that the core of our personality is formed in the first few years of our lives and it remains unchanged there after. The way we interpret life and give meaning to the happenings around us will remain unchanged throughout our lives they say.

> Alfred Adler, the pioneer of Individual Psychology, says, *by the end of the fifth year of life a child has reached a unified*

and crystallized pattern of behaviour, its own style of approach to problems and tasks. It has already fixed its deepest and most lasting conception of what to expect from the world and from itself.

After forming his own pattern of life the individual interprets and sees events and experiences according to his personal understanding of life and life situations. We know that an individual is the sumtotal of his past experiences that have influenced him according to his personal interpretation of them in conformity with the meaning he has given to his life. This personal meaning that he gives to events is based on his initial experiences and his understanding of what he felt they were at that time.

An individual's interpretations of these early experiences get embedded in his mind and stay with him in future and he perceives future experiences according to them. Even if these interpretations are erroneous and lead him to difficulty and misfortune he will fail to see where the fault lies. Whatever an event may really be, our own interpretation of it is the only truth for us. This is precisely why two people witnessing the same situation can have absolutely opposite understanding of it, and every experience further reinforces their perception.

Resistance to change or the readiness to it is based on an individual's personal pattern of interpretation. A child who grows up living with people who are flexible in their approach and have encouraged him to try new things is likely to grow up to be a creative person who is eager to adopt new ideas and thoughts. He is likely to give a positive meaning to life and will be ready to learn. His personal statement to change and learning can be something like this, 'trying new ideas is rewarding, change brings pleasure not pain' and we will find him more willing to change.

On the other hand if a child in his early years was always discouraged by the people around him, or made fun of, or rebuked when he did something on his own, will grow up not wanting to try new ideas and thoughts. He will also be less sure of himself and as such resist all change. He will want to confine himself to the security of his shell that he has built around himself. His personal statement can read something like this, 'don't attempt anything new, remain as you are, change will bring pain not pleasure'. This child, when he grows up, is likely to resist all learning and change.

If no inner change is possible, we may ask, then why should we make any attempt to change at all? Why are self help books written and read? Why do we go and listen to talks on self-improvement? Is this a total waste of effort? Do we have to just live and suffer and go?

To this, let me tell you dear reader, there is no need to despair at all. Mistakes can be corrected and set right but it takes a lot of motivation and determination on our part to be able to do so. Remember, nothing is impossible if you don't make it so, but no one else can do it for you either. Change requires a shift in our way of looking at and interpreting events and circumstances, and as such it has to be from within. The only person you can change is you yourself.

The meaning we give to an event is seldom determined by the event itself but by what we make it out to be. A little setback in a task attempted can be enough to dishearten one person and he may quit while another person may take it as a challenge, find solutions to the problems, work hard on them and emerge triumphant in the end. The difference between this opposite reaction to the same event by the two individuals, and their resultant behaviour to the same situation is the difference between their individual interpretation and the meaning given to it by them. We know that the meaning we give to life's events is determined by the way we interpreted our initial experiences before the pattern of our life had crystallized and taken shape, i.e., in our first few years of life. Mistakes in the meaning given to life can be corrected only when we acknowledge that there is a mistake in the first place and then are eager to set it right.

> Philip C. McGraw, in his book *Life Strategies*, says, *If you refuse to acknowledge your own self destructive behaviours, not only will they continue, they will actually gain momentum, become more deeply entrenched in the habitual pattern of your life, and grow more and more resistant to change.*

My friend was having problems with her marriage. She was very possessive about doing things her way. Every time her husband wanted to do things differently she felt threatened and insisted on having her way. She would throw tantrums and make life difficult for him. This attitude of hers was taking its toll. Her husband tried his best to make her understand but to no avail. My friend had had a difficult childhood where she had to fight her way through to be noticed. She was doing the same here and this was breaking up her marriage. She loved her husband well and when he threatened her with a divorce she went to a counsellor for help. He helped her to see where the mistake was, and this improved and saved their marriage.

The first step towards helping ourselves with our problems is to recognise that there is a problem. How can we help ourselves or seek help unless we know that there is something wrong with us. To be able to identify our problems and look for solutions we have to acknowledge them first. We will not take our car to a mechanic unless we know there is something wrong with it. We will continue to use it till it breaks down completely. We may even be stranded on the road. Our not acknowledging the problem will only aggravate it further.

Acknowledging a problem is half the battle won, when we know that there is something wrong with us we are more willing to change and improve. But, for this have to be prepared to reconsider the situations that led to our initial faulty understanding of them and be determined to correct them. Taking help from people who are especially trained in interpreting meanings given to life can help, but the change has to be from within. For some it may be swift and easy while for others it may take a little more time and effort but nothing is difficult or impossible for a person who values his life and himself enough. Life is too precious you know, you got the one in 300,000 billion chance, make the most of it.

People approaching middle age are also, at times, known to resist change. Middle-aged people are afraid of getting old and by resisting change they get a false sense of security. They feel that if they refuse to change they will be able to hold time. This is why some people will just refuse to change in accordance with the time, they may even refuse to dress or behave in conformity with their age. This refusal to change with age has never helped anyone; the only thing it has achieved is frustration or ridicule, or both. If you do not change with the time, time will change you but it will not be on your terms and will not be to your liking either. You will become obsolete any way.

> *The circumstances of the world are so variable, that an irrevocable purpose or opinion is almost synonymous with a foolish one.* —W. H. Seward.

There were two bakers in a market having adjoining shops. Both were doing good business and were second-generation bakers. Their products were liked by all. But slowly, and with time, tastes of the people began to change and they started asking for more variety and new products. One of the bakers was ready to experiment with new ideas and items while the other one held on to his age-old specialties. As time went by the baker who was experimenting with new technique and range started growing rapidly while the other baker started to lose business. Then came a time when he had to close the shop. He did not change with the time and got trampled.

The difference between a loser and a winner is the difference in their readiness to learn and change. If you are not satisfied with your progress you have to change your plans and do things differently. As the saying goes, 'if your today is like what your yesterday was, your tomorrow will be what your today is'. If you stick to what you have been doing you will get what you have been getting. Your future is what you do today irrespective of what you want and desire and plan. If you want to improve, you have to change.

Change does not mean losing your identity or forgetting your past, it simply means improving upon it. None of us was born perfect and none of us is perfect today. It is those who learn faster and change better are the ones who are better adapted to life. They in turn become more confident individuals and have a stronger inner self that never feels threatened by learning and change. When you learn more you get better equipped to face the challenges of life and attain success faster too.

In the following chapters we are going to look at various qualities that are needed in leading a healthier and more fulfilling life. You will imbibe these qualities in direct proportion to your readiness to learn and change where required. Just keep these few points in mind.

1. Change is the essence of life; it is inevitable and takes place every day. Make the most of it and always change for the better.
2. Remember, no progress can take place without change, the better prepared you are the faster it will be.
3. Change is possible only with your determination and understanding of your problems and your willingness to change accordingly. It is you and only you who can make it happen.
4. Resistance to change may, at times, provide a false sense of security but it will soon make you obsolete.
5. The difference between a loser and a winner is the difference in their willingness and readiness to change and improve. There can be no learning or improvement without change.

Rule
Four

Identify your Goals

Name it and
claim It.

Be specific about your aim
Know What You Want

A journey to nowhere
Will take you nowhere.

Your journey to fulfilment is propelled forward by the
goals you set along the way.—Cherie Carter-Scott.

A goal is an aim towards which our endeavour is directed; it is the destination of our journey; it is the crystallization of our dreams; it is the expression of our desires; it is giving shape to our vision. A goal is recognising and identifying our very own mission in life.

If we do not know where we are going we are bound to get lost. A journey to nowhere will take us nowhere; we need to know our destination to reach it. We have all heard tales about how people have accidentally stumbled on to gold mines and become rich, how they have fallen through rooftops and landed in palaces. But fairy tales are fairy tales and we are human beings living on this earth. In real life accidents are only known to take us to our graves, not to gold mines or palaces. The best we can expect from an accident is to escape unhurt if we are lucky, (see how luck is important here), but if we do not learn our lesson in time we may not be as lucky a second time.

To do anything we have to first identify our goal before we can start working on it. We have to know what we want to achieve before we can make any attempt do so. Doing anything and everything needs an identified goal. We can't travel without a destination, we can't shoot without an aim, we can't construct without a blueprint, we can't cook without knowing what we want to cook, we can't write without knowing what we want to write, in fact, we can't do anything without knowing what we want to do. Identifying our goal is the first step towards our destination without which the journey cannot start.

> Philip McGraw, in his book *Life Strategies*, says, *If you cannot name, and with great specificity, what is that you want, then you will never be able to step up and claim it.*

No dream can be brought to life without having been dreamt and no action can be taken without knowing what we want to achieve. For a writer getting an idea is half the work done, an idea formed in his mind works on its own, he can sleep over an idea and have it crystallized in the morning. An idea for a writer is the foundation of his goal, it tells him what to write about but he cannot write a book unless he knows and plans every detail of the book carefully. No big venture can be undertaken and executed successfully without proper planning and no planning is possible without first knowing what we are planning for.

Establishing a goal is essential to success, and the sooner we identify our goals the better it is for our progress. Children should be encouraged to set their goals early in life. Studies have shown that individuals who have had their goals set before they reached high school fared better in life. A child who knows what he wants to be as an adult will pick up a lot of relevant information along the way without his having to put extra effort into it, he will be better prepared for his goal when he grows up. Setting goals early is even more important in areas where physical training is also a part of learning; a musician who starts training early in life is likely to attain greater heights; athletes, of course, have to start young.

Providence has nothing good or high in
store for one who does not resolutely aim

at something high or good.—A purpose is
the eternal condition of success.

—T.T. Munger

Imagine a situation where a student who is about to finish school does not know what he wants to be in life, he has not identified his goal, he does not know if he wants to be a scientist or a musician, an engineer or an entrepreneur, a doctor or a lawyer, a teacher or a bureaucrat, he has no vision for his future. What do we expect him to do in a situation like this? Is it possible for him to work in any area with zeal without knowing what he wants to do? Can he pick up any significant talent or knowledge with no specific goal?

Now imagine another situation where the youngster knows well in advance that he wants to be a scientist when he grows up. How will he be different from the one we just discussed? This youngster, with his goal set, will be more focused and clear about what he wants in life. He will automatically pay more attention to science subjects, learn and retain more relevant information in science, and finish school ready with plans to enter the appropriate college for his particular field. Every step of the way he will be marching towards his goal to success, and we expect him to achieve greater heights.

All successful people have one thing in common; they have well-defined goals. Having well-defined goals provides energy and increases our efficiency. It also saves us a lot of time we would otherwise have wasted in trying to figure out what we wanted by trial and error. Trial and error learning is expensive; it extracts its own price.

The most important thing to keep in mind while establishing our goals is to see that our goals should be in accordance with our inner values and desires. They should in no way clash with our inner and deep-rooted self. If our goals are not in conformity with our inner character and we have set them under pressure of what we feel is expected of us by the people around us, if it is the external forces that have played a major part in our decision making, then we are likely to be confused, hesitant, and unsure of the correctness of our decision and we will never feel happy with our choice. This will come in the way of our achievements; we will never be able to do our best.

While setting your goals always insist on being yourself, imitating others will only bring frustration. What success means to you is important for your sense of fulfilment. If you merely follow your social pattern and expectations of achieving power, fame, and money, that are not what you value and desire, then accomplishing what is of no value to you will only bring you a feeling of emptiness within.

Our inner desires are in our sub-conscious mind and our sub-conscious mind is what we truly are, it is our unalterable self, and unless our sub-conscious mind is in tune with our conscious mind, which can be influenced by external forces, the two will not work in harmony and we will not be able to realise our full potential. The most wonderful thing about having a goal in conformity with our inner self is that in this case we do not have self-made obstacles in our way. Both our sub-conscious and our conscious minds will work along with us and this will help us in being more focused, energetic and enthusiastic about our goals. And this is what will make all the difference in our level of success and sense of achievement.

Being confused, misguided or wrong about our goals is worse than having no goal at all. Every day we come across people who have worked hard and long towards a wrong goal and then are frustrated upon attaining it. Nothing can be sadder than this and we should be careful while choosing our goals.

This is especially true in a situation where a child may aspire to go into a profession that is not perceived by the society to be as profit making in material terms as some other professions are. For example, if a youngster wants to be a painter or a writer he may come across a lot of pressure from his family and the people around him to reconsider his decision. Most people in these professions are not expected to make as much money as people in some other professions like lawyers and doctors do. But can a youngster who has his heart set on being a painter work with as much enthusiasm to be a doctor? It is likely that if he is forced by external forces to set his goal to be a doctor he will not be able to do his best. His inner desire to be an artist will keep coming in his way. Chances are that if he was allowed to become an artist he would have attained greater heights and fame, he could even have made as much money, or more, than what people in other professions do because he would then have put his whole self into achieving his goal. Besides, whatever our profession may be, there is always room at the top, and it is always beautiful from up there.

> *They build too low who build beneath the skies.* —Young.

We should, as parents and teachers help youngsters dream big and with courage. We should help them focus on their dreams and aspirations without reservations. I would tell any youngster who came to me for help in identifying his goal to sit back and reflect on what will make him really happy? What he thinks he will really like to be? I would tell him to imagine God to be standing in front of him and asking him to choose his goal. What would it be then? Whatever comes to his mind now he should visualise and see if that is what he really wants, and if he is satisfied with it, he should go ahead and make it his goal. He will then, in all probability, be able to attain his chosen goal with success as it will then be in conformity with his inner desires and aspirations. Excellence in every profession is rewarding and fulfilling irrespective of whether you are a doctor, an engineer, a scientist, a writer, a musician, a lawyer, or a business executive.

> *No bird soars too high if he soars with his*
> *own wings.* —W. Blake.

Goals set later in life can also do wonders, they have done so for many, they will do that for you too, but the only thing is that you cannot get back the time lost in arriving at your goals late. But as the saying goes, 'better late than never', it is better to arrive late than not to arrive at all. In arriving late you could have gathered a few valuable experiences on your way, and if you are smart enough you can make use of them here. You can work faster and better towards your goal. Your wisdom and efficiency gained over time can help you here, provided you are smart enough to make use of them.

All highly successful people have well-defined goals and they work with determination and dedication towards achieving them. They surrender themselves completely to their work and this is what makes them successful.

Set your goals with courage and work on them with conviction. Nothing is impossible for a determined man. Always aim big and never be afraid of setting your sight high. You will reach the height of your sight. Make sure it is high enough for you.

> *Aim at the sun, and you may not reach it; but your arrow will fly much higher than if aimed at an object on the level with yourself.* —J. Hawes.

Identifying your goal is not enough in itself, it has to be planned and executed as well. Planning is an important part of your goal setting. If it is a big venture it may need to be done in phases. Every detail has to be planned and the sequence in which the work has to be done worked out. Even something as simple as a long journey has to be planned in phases, it has to be done in parts. We will have to plan how much distance we can cover in one day, where we will stay for the night, what time we want to leave the next day so that we can cover the planned distance for that day, how many days it will take us, where do we want to stay on our way, and so on. If we just pick up our car and start moving without planning we run a high risk of getting into trouble.

We can also fix targets for various stages of our growth. Fixing targets is a very good way to keep going, it improves our efficiency. Targets motivate us into action and meeting our targets is like achieving small victories on our way to success. This in turn brings its own rewards in the form of energising us and keeping us focused. When I was doing a weekly column for a paper the Editor told me to send my work by Friday every week, but I set my target for Wednesday. I was able to meet my target without fail no matter how busy I was. Sending my work early gave me a sense of satisfaction and the freedom to pursue other things as well without the pressure of an approaching deadline. If you look at it closely, working Wednesday to Wednesday is the same as working Friday to Friday, the only difference is that you do not have the pressure of a deadline hanging on your head and you also have the satisfaction of having met your target, and this helps in your efficiency and performance.

Targets help us to discipline ourselves too. This is especially true with long-term goals and big projects. In the case of long-term goals nothing is urgent but everything is important and the difference between a successful and a not so successful person is that a successful individual does not get absorbed in urgent everyday matters losing sight of what is really important to him in the long run, while the common man gets carried away by the urgent things of life demanding his immediate attention.

Urgent everyday matters can be as trivial as a phone call or some urgent household chore, but more important things like studying for our exams or writing a book are rarely urgent but are equally important, these are also the things that are important for success. By setting targets we keep important things into focus and they do not get pushed aside by matters that may not be crucial to success.

Goals can also not wait endlessly to be accomplished. Opportunities have a time limit and we have to honour it. If you want to enter into a certain business but if you wait for too long the market may get saturated making it impossible for you to accomplish your dream.

However much we may have planned and prepared for our journey towards our goals there might still be times when we may not be able to go about our plans the way we planned, we may need to alter our plans. For example, if a tree falls in a storm and blocks our way we will not stand there waiting for the tree to be removed before we proceed further, we will take a detour and go. A detour is just a different road to the same destination and we should not hesitate to take it where required. Our destination is important not the route, change it if it is wise to do so.

Setting a goal is the key to success. Look at the successful people around you and see how they set their goals with clarity and thought, phase them out, set targets, work on them, and march towards their goals attaining success all the way. There is no reason why you cannot do that too. Just revise these tips before you move further.

1. Goals are essential for success. Setting a goal is an essential part of your planning.
2. Goals should be in accordance with your inner desires and aspirations. They have to be in conformity with your inner self.
3. Always aim high. You will reach the height of your sight.
4. Setting goals early in life saves time and energy. You should try and set your goals as early as possible.
5. Goals need to be planned and executed with dedication and hard work. You have to be focused on your goals to attain significant success.
6. Setting targets helps us in realising our goals more easily.

Rule
Five

Take Challenges

Failures are
lessons
on our way to
success

Be Prepared to Fail

Take enough Risks

Success is a challenge well met,
The number of attempts do not count.

Failure is, in a sense, the highway to success,
inasmuch as every discovery of what is false
leads us to seek earnestly after what is true,
and every fresh experience points out some
form of error which we shall afterwards
carefully avoid. —Keats.

If you want to be successful in life you have to be courageous enough to handle failure. No endeavour can ever guarantee success, and if you are afraid of failure, you will not be able to take any risks. Those who are afraid of failures never fail, they simply never try. You will fail only when you do something. You can't achieve anything worthwhile unless you are prepared to take a few risks.

When you take risks you come out of your comfort zone and try something that is new to you and does not guarantee success. It is listening to your gut feeling, to your inner voice, to the singing of your heart. It does not mean being foolhardy, it simply means taking calculated chances of success.

The word risk itself means the possibility of incurring misfortune or loss, and setbacks are a fact of life, what is important here is whether we have the capability of learning from our mistakes and moving ahead or not? When we learn from our mistakes they become stepping-stones on our way to success.

> Thomas Edison has said, *I am not discouraged, because every wrong attempt discarded is another step forward.* Edison is said to have tried 10,000 times before he was finally successful with the light bulb.

Facing challenges is essential to success and if we have not faced enough challenges it is likely that we have not done anything much in life either. It is better to attempt and fail than not to attempt at all. If you do not make an attempt you fail anyway, because of not having tried. A sleeping man never fails, except in life.

He alone is exempt from failure who makes no effort. —Whatley

We all know that it is better to try and fail than not to try at all but how many of us are really able to do it? Rather than take a challenge, most of us will like to stay within the secure walls of mediocrity getting 'walled' in the process. This way we ensure that we never reach the top. Not being able to take risks is a guarantee to a life of mediocrity. We can't take risks without coming out of our security network and we can't rise unless we break this net.

Walt Disney had to declare bankruptcy five times before he became successful.

John Grisham was not discouraged even after a number of publishers turned down his work. He has eighty million books in print all over the world today.

When we encounter a setback or a failure we have two options, either to get defeated and bow out, or to learn from the experience and move ahead, and with greater determination. The choice of the winner is obvious; he will move ahead a more experienced, learned, and confident man.

Always remember that the other side of risk is the possibility of gain, which we should look forward to. By not taking risks we lose this opportunity without giving it a try, we accept failure for ourselves and we fail.

Why then, you may ask, are we afraid of taking risks? The answer is simple, because we are not courageous enough to handle failure if it comes our way, we are not sure of our capacity to learn from our mistakes, and like the overpraised child we think if we do not make an attempt we will be able to fool ourselves and others into believing that we did not make it big not because of any fault of our's, but because we just did not try. This way we feel we will be able to hold on to the 'smart guy' label we put on ourselves though we pay heavily for it in the process; it costs us our success. The fact is, taking a risk is no risk at all, it is a chance we give ourselves, take it. You will either be successful or become wiser, you win both ways.

Taking risks requires courage, it requires faith in ourselves and our ability to take a challenge; it requires trust in our wisdom and in our judgement; it requires confidence in ourselves and our potential along with the knowledge that even if we are not successful, it will not be the end of us, we will be able to learn whatever has to be learnt from our setbacks, and emerge triumphant in the end. It requires the confidence that we will be able to bounce back come what may; it requires trust that even if we fail we will become tougher and wiser and better prepared to face a new challenge; it requires assurance that this will not be the end of our opportunities, there will be many more challenges waiting for us in future. And above all, it requires confidence that public opinion about our failures will not affect us and destroy our zeal. How else could Wright Brothers give us our airplane?

When we come across people who have not been successful in life we find that they are the people who are most afraid of taking risks. They have made themselves failure proof; they take no risks. You can't fall from the bottom they know, and this gives them a sense of security they want. They have all kinds of excuses for not attempting anything big, and they have all kinds of reasons for not having been able to do so. They will find themselves a victim of every conceivable misfortune and they will blame their mediocrity on just anything they can think of, be it unfavourable circumstances, bad health, bad luck, bad partners, lack of talent, lack of opportunity, inconsiderate bosses, market recession and what not, every imaginable excuse is good enough for them, it keeps them from taking risks. And one thing is sure; they will always blame external forces for their misfortunes, they will never acknowledge their own role in it. Blaming others does nothing for them except absolving them of their responsibility in their self inflicted misfortune.

On the other hand, look at the successful people around you. See how they have been taking risks all the way to their success. They have had no better guarantee of success than you or anyone has had, on the contrary they have, in fact, faced more failures than you have simply because they took more risks. But they have had more successes as well, because they took those risks. And that is all that matters at the end of the day. The world sees their success and so do they. Do we care to know how many unsuccessful attempts it took for man to learn to fly, or for Edison to come up with the light bulb?

Abraham Lincoln is one man we all know as one of the most successful presidents of the United States of America but how many of us know of how and where he failed before he could finally achieve what he set out to achieve. He failed in business at the ages of twenty-one and twenty-four; he lost his sweetheart at twenty-six; he had a nervous breakdown at twenty-seven; he lost a congressional race at thirty-four and a senatorial race at forty-five; he failed to become the vice-president at forty-seven; he lost senatorial race again at forty-nine; and after all this he was finally elected the President of the United States at fifty-two. And this is all we know, and care about. The history of US would have been different had Lincoln bowed down to his setbacks and failures.

Another major difference between a successful man and an average individual is that the successful man treats every failure as a lesson for success. He learns from his mistakes and moves ahead. Remember, if you do not learn from your mistakes you will be condemned to repeat them. All men make mistakes; only fools repeat them. Mistakes are like a stubborn child; they won't let go of you till you listen to them.

Taking risks is not always as risky as it may appear to be. There is a difference in being foolhardy and taking calculated risks. Taking a well-researched risk is always a good investment but it requires faith in one's ability to be successful and also the confidence that if misfortune does strike, it will not be the end. If you do not have enough courage to be able to handle failure you will not be able to take any risk however much you may know that the odds are in your favour and you stand a very good chance of success. Have the courage to fail and you will succeed.

Challenge is a part of life; if you do not take it you let go of some part of your life with it. Lee Iacocca was fired by Henry Ford at the age of fifty-four but he went and joined a failing Chrysler and became a legend by making it a success. Iacocca did not bow down to adversity and this is what made him a legend.

Now the question that naturally comes to mind here is, when does one know that it is time to take his risk? When does one know he is not being foolhardy? When does one know it is wise to take the risk? To this, let me tell you, the time to take your risk is when you feel it is the right time for you, when you are consumed with the desire to take the plunge, when you feel you are ready for the challenge, when you know what you are in for, when you have studied and calculated the risk, when you are prepared for the consequences whatever they may be, and when your inner self tells you so. The best time to take your risk is when your heart tells you to.

Just a few words of advice can help you to plan your risk better. First make sure that this is what your heart and soul really desire, this is what you really want. Visualise your dream in your mind; see that it stirs you from inside; make sure you know everything you have to know about how to make your dream come true; make sure you have planned for the resources you will need for the venture; know how much time it will take; plan for the consequences just in case it does not turn out your way; and above all, have faith in yourself and know that nothing is impossible to the courageous and the determined. Caution is not to make you apprehensive but to make you more confident.

Failure is too harsh a word to use to define misfortune in an evdeavour. The word *failure* speaks of an unsuccessful end of an attempt, but there are no ends in life. Life is a continuous process; both success and failure are a part of life, a passing phase. No unsuccessful attempt should be perceived as a *failure*, it should, instead, be seen as a setback, a mistake, a blunder, an error and a lesson for our future success. These are words that give us hope and the possibility to learn, they help us to see how we could be responsible for what happened and how we can set it right for the future. Knowing that there is a mistake gives hope, and mistakes can be rectified. It is human to make mistakes, but it is divine to learn from them. The best thing that mistakes do for us is to make us wiser, stronger, tougher and better prepared to proceed on our way to success. Always remember, *failure* is a lesson and nothing more, and no learning is a waste and we are here to learn.

Just know this when you attempt your risks,

1. Taking risks is essential to success, the more risks you take the better chances of success you have.
2. It is better to attempt and fail than not to try at all. When you make an attempt you have a chance, when you don't you have no chance at all.

3. When you learn from your failures they pave the way to success.
4. The best time to take a risk is when your heart tells you to.
5. Take failure as a challenge; treat it as a mistake, an error, and a lesson and you will not be afraid of it.
6. Above all, always remember, taking a risk is no risk at all, it is an opportunity you give yourself. Take it.

Rule
Six

Conquer Your Limits

If you can't run,
use a bike.

Turn Minus into Plus

Convert Loss into Gain

The wise will turn the tide,
The fool will drown.

If you have a lemon, make a lemonade. —Dale Carnegie

We can do anything we want to if we stick to it long
enough. —Helen Keller

The school records of Nobel Prize winning physicist and author Richard Feynman (1918-1987) show that he had an IQ of 124, 'just above average'. His wife recalled that he was delighted with this revelation. 'To win a Nobel Prize was no big deal', he said, 'but to win it with an IQ of 124—*that* was something.'

Man is the only species gifted with the power to go beyond his limits. Man is not ruling this planet for any other reason but his unique ability to conquer his boundaries. Man was certainly not endowed with the ability to fly while some other species could so beautifully do so, but today it is he who has conquered the skies and even ventured into space like no other known species can. He is not even the fastest runner on this planet but it is he who has mastered speed. He cannot survive in water but he has ventured into the depth of the ocean and is capable of spending days submerged in water. Man has never placed limits on himself, and the successful individual has learnt his lesson from him.

The famous psychologist Alfred Adler was a great advocate of this extraordinary power of the human being to be able to compensate for his shortcomings. The most extra-ordinary human quality according to him is man's ability to *turn minus into plus*, to be able to overcome his limitations. It is this quality that makes man unique and superior to all in spite of his very human limitations.

Man does not have the ability to survive in the jungles like most animals can, he cannot live in the wild like them and hope to survive for one whole year, his body is not strong enough to tolerate the extremes of temperature, his digestive system cannot digest various raw foods, he is not strong enough to fight wild animals and also runs the risk of being eaten up by them if he is not careful, and yet it is he who is the master of them all. All this was possible because he had this unique ability to overcome his limitations and turn them into his strengths.

As Dale Carnegie has said, *the most important thing in life is not to capitalise on your gains. Any fool can do that. The really important thing is to profit from your losses. That requires intelligence; and it makes the difference between a man of sense and a fool.*

Cashing on your assets is nothing great, just anyone can do it. The lion is the king of the jungle not because of any special quality of his, but only because nature made him powerful enough to kill and eat the weaker animals. The big fish can eat the small fish just because it is big. But man has not conquered the skies because he can fly; he has conquered the skies in spite of his inability to fly. He has used his brains and found ways to fly at the greatest known speed and is now improving on it further. To be able to turn minus into plus is what is unique to man.

Success comes to the man who knows how to turn the tide in his favour, who knows how to overcome his limitations, who knows how to find solutions. This ability to turn minus into plus is what is most important for success. In no situation do we have everything lined up in our favour to go and grab an opportunity, our path is always laid out with certain problems and limitations and it is he who can handle them best will succeed.

Undertaking any new venture brings with it its own set of problems that have to be tackled and solved and this is where the difference between a winner and a loser lies. A winner is always the one who takes on a challenge and finds solutions; who is not defeated by failures, and even if he fails and falls, he does not stay on the ground for long, he soon bounces back, and with greater strength. He is successful in doing whatever he wants to do irrespective of the obstacles in his way.

You place a winner in any adversity, you give him any handicap, you put any limits on him still he will emerge successful come what may. The key to success is not just the ability to harness gains but the ability to harness gains from losses. The one who can turn losses into gains is the one who will win in the end. When Lee Iacocoa joined Chrysler, the company had announced a loss of almost 160 million dollars. How he turned the company around is no secret and this is what makes him one of the best known winners of all. How many people do you think could have turned such a huge loss into gain, or even dared to try?

And let me tell you that no one is a born winner; all of us have to learn to win. You cannot be the best runner unless you have practised enough, built your stamina, had a regular training schedule, worked on it the way your coach told you to, and above all, put your whole self into it.

Conquering your limitations is especially true where we find people with certain handicaps excelling in areas we would normally not expect them to venture into. We come across painters without arms who paint with their feet and win acclaim. They hold the brush in their toes, or by mouth, and they produce beautiful paintings that are able to challenge painters with both hands. Then there is this talented dancer and actress from the South with an artificial leg who refused to quit after her accident in which she lost one leg. She was devastated by this tragedy for some time but she gradually recovered from her shock and with determination learnt to dance with her artificial leg. She has made an inspiring movie on her misfortune and how she overcame it with her willpower. Handicaps and misfortunes can limit you only as long as you allow them to.

Most of the blind develop a very keen sense of touch and sound, many of them become singers of great talent. They compensate for lack of one sense by developing another better. The deaf and dumb have become painters of fame. Beethoven too composed some of his best music after he became deaf. The success of Helen Keller is a marvel in itself without a parallel till date.

To be a winner we must know that nothing is impossible when handled with determination and will, our limitations can limit us only as far as we let them, it is our choice and we are the masters of our situations and the makers of their outcomes. We shape our own destiny.

Just remember,

1. Always know that it is only man who has this unique power to turn his weaknesses into strengths.
2. If you do not set any limits on your self you won't have any.
3. Harnessing your profits is no big deal; anyone can do it. Turning losses into profits is what makes you a winner.
4. Finally, nothing is impossible to the determined man.

Rule
Seven

Take Initiative

To run
you have to
stand first.

Act. Get Going.

Get started

If you do not tell your feet to run,
They won't.

To initiate means to start, to make the first move, to make a beginning. Nothing gets started without a start. No journey can commence without taking the first step; no house can be built without laying the first brick; no writing can be done without writing the first word and no planning can be done without the first thought. To initiate is to start action and every action needs a start and every work done has had a beginning. We can't reach 'the end' without 'the beginning'. Anything that moves; anything that grows; any plan that has been carried out; any project that has taken shape; any book that has been written; any painting that has been painted, in fact just anything that has been done has had a start and someone has taken the initiative to do it.

Getting ideas, setting goals, thinking positive, thinking big, all make good sense but without action they mean nothing. However good an idea may be if it is not acted upon, it never works. It is like having a Rolls-Royce without the keys. You can only look at it and sigh. Having great ideas that have not been acted upon can only bring pain not pleasure.

> Stephen R Covey, in his book *The Seven Habits Of Highly Effective People*, says, *The difference between people who exercise initiative and those who don't is literally the difference between night and day. I am not talking about a 25 to 50 percent difference in effectiveness; I'm talking about a 5000-plus percent difference, particularly if they are smart, aware, and sensitive to others.*

The biggest obstacle on our way to success is our hesitation to make a start. We may have great plans that have been studied and worked out in great detail, but if we do not work on them they can be of no use to us except to be sorry reminders of wasted time, lost opportunities, and unrealised goals.

> Confucius has said, *To see what is right and not to do it, is want of courage.*

If I want to set up a big business of my own and for that I have studied and planned everything in detail; the market, the place, the resources, the phases of growth, the targets, the prospects, the time it will take and have everything ready but if I keep postponing to initiate the venture it will not get started, and if I do not start it I will achieve nothing but frustration. There is nothing more frustrating than inaction, and no amount of planning is worth anything if it has not been acted upon. A small dream accomplished is better than a big dream dreamt.

In everyday life we come across many such situations where a good idea never got materialised for want of initiative. A friend of mine once told me how she wanted to quit her job and go into a business of her own. She was working for a garment export company and knew the tricks of the trade well. She knew everything that needed to be known and was well-equipped to have an export house of her own. When I met her again after a gap of five years she was still working on her job and her dream of having her own business was still a dream. Her only accomplishment till then was that her enthusiasm and confidence had diminished considerably. When I asked her the reason for this delay she said, 'Mridula, you know, how busy I am, I just never got the opportunity to quit my job and venture on my own, I have family commitments you know, my husband is a busy man and we need my salary, if I start my own business I will have to put in longer and uncertain hours and it will also take some time before I can go into profit, and I cannot afford that you know.' My friend is waiting for the right time to get started, she thinks she cannot afford to quit her job at this point of time; she is unable to realise that her job is proving to be too expensive for her. It is costing her her dream.

A more determined person in a similar situation would have found ways of planning her time better, cut down on her expenses or arranged for a loan which she could repay after the business went into profit, she could have hired help or asked her husband to take time out if he could, and then taken the plunge and reaped her harvest. The reasons my friend had for her inability to carry out her plans were similar to what a lot of us have, and beautiful plans get wasted. But there are also a few enterprising people who are able to find solutions to such everyday problems, they are able to take their challenge, and in most cases they succeed. The most common handicap in not being able to realise one's potential is not lack of opportunity or vision, but lack of initiative.

The number one dampener of initiative is lack of confidence in one's ability to get one's idea through. This is typically true of people with a lot of talent who are working in secure jobs. They want to venture out on their own but are never able to do so, their dreams are always a distant possibility to be realised some day, but that day is never today. They are always hesitating to jump into the fray. They are not sure of their ability to handle the problems they may encounter on their way and they never do. They have a secure job, a comfortable home, and a loving family, they want to make it big in this world, but are afraid to disturb the smooth running of their lives; they are afraid of the unknown and are unable to bring themselves together to get started on their ambitious plans. Their dreams always remain dreams, only to frustrate them in later years.

> *A great deal of talent is lost in this world*
> *for the want of a little courage.*
> —Sydney Smith.

The best builder of confidence is action, the best generator of ideas is action, the best way to reach your goal is action, and the best way to make your dream come true is also action. Action leads to action, this is the law of motion. It is unchangeable and universal.

Every success is an idea acted upon and every successful person is a man of action. The achiever acts and the non-achiever stalls action. The achiever says ' here and now', the non-achiever says 'some other time, some other day'. If today is not the right day for you then tomorrow will also not be so. Life is a continuous process, if you have one set of problems today you will have another set of problems tomorrow. If you want to wait for all your problems to be sorted out before you undertake your project, your wait will never end.

The man of action is the one who will find ways of doing things no matter how difficult they may be, or what obstacles he may encounter. The saying, 'where there is a will there is a way' is for him and he firmly believes in 'what you want to do you can do', and also 'what you want to do today do it now.' The non-action man too will tell you how he understands this doctrine and is always keen to follow it, but he will also tell you that there is no way in which he can do it now. He always feels helpless in the face of adversity, be it real or perceived, and above all, today is never the right day for him. And, we all know, as well as he does; his tomorrow never comes.

Life is a continuous process and so are opportunities and difficulties. We can never wait for the right time; we have to create it for ourselves. We have to look for opportunities and start working on them. Difficulties can be solved when they arrive but opportunities once missed may be lost forever.

You can't start walking till you stand up and take the first step; you can't write till you pick up a pen and put it to paper; your fan won't work till you switch it on; you can't cook till you light the gas; you can't work till you lift your hand. Nothing will get done till you take the initiative to do it. Writers are said to have phases of mental block, times when they are unable to get ideas to write, but every writer can meet his deadline if he picks up a pen and starts writing.

Procrastination is the best friend of hesitation. The more you postpone the more hesitant you become. If you are afraid of facing a situation don't postpone it, just go and tackle it, and when you do so you will find yourself relaxed and confident for having accomplished a difficult task. If you are feeling hesitant about going to the bank for a loan for your new project your hesitation will not help you in any way. The more you postpone the more apprehensive you will become. Just walk into the bank and talk to the Bank Manager, there is a possibility that you will come out successful, and even if you are not, you will be more confident and relaxed for having tried any way. Making an attempt is a reward in itself and even if you are not successful the first time it gives you a little more experience in handling a similar situation in future. By making an attempt you win both ways, you either get what you want, or you become wiser.

The one sure way to getting things done is not to postpone getting started. If you are having self-doubts, go through your plans again, see if there is something that is worrying you and needs your attention, set it right and proceed. Get started. You may feel hesitant or unsure of yourself in the beginning but when you persist you will soon find that you are increasingly getting in control of the situation and gaining confidence. You will soon find yourself marching towards your goal and to success

People can generally be classified in two categories, some are leaders others are followers. Leaders, as can be known by the very nature of their quality, are few and far between, the rest are followers. Leaders are people with courage, are always ready to make the first move, they lead. They are sure of themselves and their capacity to get things done, they are not afraid to take the first step, and, as such, are ahead of others. The followers are hesitant people, less sure of themselves, never willing to try anything new, they feel more confident when they tread on the beaten path, they follow. They lack the confidence that it takes to be the first, and they never are. Most of us belong to this category.

> Jacques Maritain says, *A coward flees backward, away from new things. A man of courage flees forward, in the midst of new things.*

Look at all the successful people around you, see how they take initiative in everything they do. Successful people do not stand by waiting for someone else to come forward and help them, rather it is they who will come forward and help others where possible. As the saying goes, if you want to get anything done give it to the busiest man. A busy man is a man of action; it is he who will be able to get your work done too, not the one who is himself waiting for his work to be done by someone else. The successful *are* busy, the unsuccessful *feel* busy. The successful have time for everything; the unsuccessful will never have time for anything. If next time you feel you do not have time for what you want to do just stop and see if it is an excuse for inaction.

Excuse is the worst enemy of initiative. Instead of working on his plan the non-achiever will list any number of reasons for being unable to do his task in spite of all his good intentions. He will tell you how his responsibilities are coming in his way, how his job leaves little time for him to pursue his goals, how his health won't permit him, how his spouse is not cooperating, how his boss is bossing over him, etc. All these reasons for inaction, according to him, are beyond his control and he feels helpless. The only way to get out of this mindset is to look at the situation straight in the eye and go ahead and get started.

The best way to make your dreams come true is to wake up and sprint. Always remember it is you, and only you, who has to make the start.

Just keep a few of these tips in mind and get going.

1. Be a man of action; do not hesitate to take the first step. Every 'end' has to have a 'beginning'.
2. If you want to be a leader take the first step and start moving.
3. A good idea has no meaning unless it has been acted upon. It is better to build a small cottage than to build castles in the air.
4. The worst enemy of initiative is lack of courage and getting started is the best way to overcome it.
5. Do today what you plan for tomorrow and see how it works wonders.

Rule
Eight

Accept Yourself

When you
accept yourself
the world
accepts you

Build Self Esteem
Not a swollen Head

A swollen head is like being obese,
It shows how sick you are.

Oftentimes nothing profits more than self-esteem,
grounded on what is just and right.—Milton.

We are all born unique; no two individuals are alike. Honouring and respecting this uniqueness is what esteem is all about. Self-esteem is how we look at ourselves, how comfortable we are within. It is our self-concept, our personal perception in our mind's inner eye. It is the grading we give ourselves; it is the confidence we have in our abilities; it is our opinion of self and our individuality. How comfortable we are with ourselves has a direct bearing on our performance in every area of our lives.

Having high self-esteem is not only desirable but also necessary for achieving success and being happy. No one can feel successful and happy unless he has a healthy respect for self, and no one can achieve meaningful success unless he has confidence in his capabilities. If we do not have high self-esteem we will not be able to respect our work and ourselves.

Having high self-esteem does not mean having a bloated ego, or being arrogant and obnoxious with a swollen head, it simply means being satisfied and contented with being what we are. When you are happy with yourself you work with confidence. A swollen head on the other hand is the result of an insecure inner self that is craving to project itself big without being sure of its real worth.

> *Behind everyone who behaves as if he were superior to others, we can suspect a feeling of inferiority, which calls for a very special effort of concealment.* —Alfred Adler

A swollen head is, in fact, a reaction to low self-esteem. When a man tries to hide his feelings of inferiority he behaves big and tries to feel superior to all. An individual who is conscious of his short height will try and walk tall by stretching himself up; a plain Jane who feels threatened in front of beautiful women will take extra care to dress well; a man who is not sure of people listening to him will talk loudly.

There is a Russian proverb that says, *Men carry their superiority inside, animals outside.*

Self-esteem is knowing your truth and honouring it, it is being content with one's self as an individual who is special and unique. I know of a young man, who is too short to be called handsome, but he is least bothered about this quality of his, he treats it as his special feature, which it really is. This acceptance of his reality helps him in feeling confident as a person and he does not have to try and stretch himself for nothing. When you are in a situation like this, and you have the confidence to say, 'yes I am short and would have liked to be tall if I had the choice, but this is not so, and I am happy as I am,' how much more confident and happy you would be. At the same time if you denied the reality that the society finds height a more desirable trait you would go into unnecessary denial and achieve nothing. Honouring your truth is not denial but acceptance of what you are and with respect.

When we come into this world we come here with our very own set of traits that may or may not be in accordance with the qualities most sought after in the social set-up we live in. Here I am not talking of any criminal disposition that an individual may claim to have inherited through his genes, we know that criminal tendencies are seldom transmitted, I am talking of qualities that are individual characteristics of his, like his IQ, looks, physical attributes, strengths, the country, class and race he belongs to etc. They may not be the best according to the standards his society has set, but these are his individual traits that make him unique and he should learn to respect his uniqueness.

> Giles has wisely said, *Esteem cannot be where there is no confidence; and there can be no confidence where there is no respect.*

We, as individuals, have our own interests, requirements, qualities and priorities. We should learn to honour and respect them, only then will we be able to truly love and respect ourselves. The best way to honour yourself is to accept who you are, where you are and what you are. If you cannot respect yourself who else can? No one else can accept you better than you can. Seeking acceptance from others will not only be a futile exercise, it will also take its toll on you, and it will drain you of your energies and limit your choices. It is more satisfying to be a beautiful flowering bush than to be an ugly tree.

We often come across people from the socially underprivileged class trying to compensate for their perceived misfortune by going out of their way to dress and behave in a manner more acceptable to their privileged peers, but in doing so they are never able to achieve the desired result, and this puts unnecessary strain on them. By trying to be different from what they really are they also run the risk of looking phoney and be made fun of. Had they honoured their truth and accepted it, as it is, they would have found themselves easily accepted by others, more confident of themselves, and better equipped to pursue their chosen goals without the extra burden of trying to be what they are not.

> As Addison says, *The chief ingredients in the composition of those qualities that gain esteem and praise, are good nature, truth, good sense, and good breeding.*

A plain looking woman dressed up in her own style, looking confident of herself who knows and accepts her truth is bound to be more impressive and attractive than her more beautiful counterpart who is not comfortable with herself. Remember, no one can make you feel inferior without your own consent.

> According to Rochefoucauld, *Esteem has more ongoing charm than friendship and even love—it captivates hearts better, and never makes ingrates.*

This does not mean that one ha[s] deny the qualities in others, or refuse [...] faults, which is necessary for learning [...] means to accept oneself as one is, le[...] what is good in others and move ahea[d] never feels threatened by looking at his own mistakes; his confidence in himself is there to protect him. He is also better prepared to look at the qualities of others, learn from them where required, and equip himself better. It is easy for him to shed his own faults and inculcate the good qualities of his fellow men. What you appreciate in others rubs on you too. Only a man with high self-esteem can learn, improve, and change easily.

Imagine a situation where you are making a public speech, you are essentially reading out a written text prepared by someone else and do not have any clear idea of what you are talking of, or reading about to your audience, and now the audience wants to discuss your talk with you. What will your reaction be? You will try to evade all questions because you will feel threatened by them and you will want to cut every one short. You may also snap at them in your frustration. You do this because you do not want to let your audience know that you were not prepared for this talk. On the other hand, had you prepared your own text, were sure of what you

aying, and had enough knowledge of your subject
a would have welcomed all discussion on your talk and
enjoyed it too. Confidence is necessary to open your
mind. It is only when we are in tune with our inner self
that we can open up to the world of learning and improving.

If you are unable to accept yourself you will look for
others to accept you. In trying to seek acceptance from
others you will deviate from the path of your progress.
Your decisions will get influenced by what you think
others want from you, not by what you think is right for
you. And the more you deviate from your path the more
it will make you like yourself less, and your entire endeavour
will be on the useless side of life. Seeking acceptance from
others will do nothing but drain your energies and limit
your choices. To be accepted by others you have to
accept yourself first.

> The wise man endeavours to shine in
> himself, the fool to outshine others. The
> wise man is happy when he gains his own
> approbation, and the fool when he
> recommends himself to the applause of
> those about him.   —Addison.

Research has shown that if we praise kids too much,
especially for qualities that are not in them in the hope

of encouraging them they become praise-dependent to boost their self-esteem and this hampers their growth. Praise is an external force that is not in your hands, you have to depend on others for it, and however much you may feel you deserve it, you may still not get it. We are least expected to shower praise on those who seek it the most.

Confidence is an internal need and it is in your control, you can build it in yourself, but remember confidence needs a solid base; you can't fool yourself into it. Moreover, praise is an external force, and external forces can never satisfy internal needs. Overpraised kids become praise-dependent, which in turn makes them a tool in the hands of forces beyond their control. They are always seeking praise from the outside world to boost their confidence in themselves, and this affects the choices they make and it stalls their growth as well.

Rochefoucauld puts it straight when he says,
If we have not peace within ourselves, it is vain to seek it from the outward sources.
The same law applies to self-esteem also.

Praise-dependent youngsters tend to become arrogant too, they want to be praised for everything they do, and if they do not get it they boast about their achievements, real or imaginary, and this comes in their path of success. Arrogance can never replace self-esteem and we should realise the subtle and glaring difference.

> When you trust yourself, you discover your truth. When you honour that truth, you can see your authentic path. Following your authentic path will lead you to the vision of prosperity that ultimately will engage your mind, ignite your heart, and cause your soul to sing. —Cherie Carter-Scott.

High self-esteem is an asset, a swollen head is a liability; one is a positive trait, and the other a negative one. Esteem is acceptance of reality; arrogance is denial of reality and the two can never meet.

Just keep these points in mind before you proceed further.

1. Always have a high regard for yourself. Do not be arrogant with a swollen head. Have a healthy regard for what you are.
2. Having high self-esteem is knowing your truth and honouring it. It is knowing that you are unique in this world; you do not have to be anything else.

3. Never try to be what you are not. It will bring pain · not pleasure.

4. Looking for praise and acceptance from others should not affect your choices.

5. Outside forces can never satisfy inner needs. When you respect yourself less you look at others to accept you, but always remember, no one can respect you more than you do yourself.

Rule
Nine

Be Disciplined

If you honour your
commitments,
they will
honour you.

Honour your Commitments

Be in control of yourself

He who is his own master
Has no master.

Most powerful is he who has himself
in his own power.—Seneca.

If you cannot be taken for your word, you cannot have much meaning. When you commit to something you are expected to stay committed. No commitment has any significance unless it is honoured. A commitment is a pledge; an obligation, a promise that has to be kept and this restricts freedom, and discipline is all about limitations. To be disciplined is to be refined too.

When you honour your commitments, either to yourself or to others, you become disciplined. It is easier to honour your commitments to others as they put restrictions on you and can question you or even take you to court for your lapse, if required. But to honour commitments to oneself takes more dedication and determination. There is no one to question or compel you and as such you tend to take it easy and can fall short of your promise. No meaningful success can result out of indiscipline. If you cannot control yourself you cannot control others too.

> *Those who command themselves, command others.* —Hazlitt.

Self-discipline is to follow your own rules, to obey the dictates of your mind, to have control over yourself. It is your ability to do what needs to be done, when it needs to be done, as it needs to be done. It is your strength to honour your resolve and do what you have decided to do even when you do not want to do it then.

Discipline is getting up at 4 in the morning to finish your assignment on time; it is practising your music lesson in the evening when your friends are out in the fields playing football; it is following the doctor's advise and not eating foods that are harmful for your health; it is refraining from buying something you want to buy when you are on a tight budget.

A disciplined person feels, and always is, in control of himself and his surroundings. Self-discipline is essential for proper growth and success. If we are not disciplined we will not be able to pursue our goals the way we would want to, our other priorities would keep coming in our way.

> *For want of self-restraint many men are engaged all their lives in fighting with difficulties of their own making, and rendering success impossible by their own cross-grained ungentleness, whilst others may be much less gifted, make their way and achieve success by simple patience, equanimity, and self control.* —Smiles.

Indiscipline can be our worst enemy. If we are not properly disciplined we will find adhering to our schedules difficult, we will not be able to force ourselves to be focused on our goals. But indiscipline is a symptom, not the disease, though we very often confuse it to be the main problem. Every day we come across people who tell us that the real obstacle on their way to success is that they are not self-disciplined, that they are not able to do what they really want to do, when they want to do, as they want to do. That other important things take their time and energy and they are unable to focus on what they want for themselves. They feel they are victims either of time, or circumstances, or their own in-disciplined self.

> *No man is free who cannot command himself.* —Pythagoras.

I too was lacking in self-discipline at one time and it cost me a number of useful years to learn my lesson, to know and understand my real problem. I had been writing for newspapers for sometime, I did it off and on for a few years but I did not have a fixed time schedule for my writing. I did it as and when I liked. I knew that one could achieve nothing substantial in writing unless one had a daily schedule that one adhered to with conviction, but I had no time schedule of my own. Chatting on the phone, going out to kitty parties, watching TV, visiting neighbours was more important to me than my work. I thought I could get away by being *a little flexible*. I would find excuses for not being able to do what I had planned for the day though deep inside I knew that this was not right, but I was helpless, and this was hampering my work. I was writing at random and that was it. Forcing myself to be more focused did not work. I did not know at that time that I was working on the symptom not the disease. How could it help?

The main problem with discipline is not indiscipline but disrespect, disrespect for yourself and your work. Disrespect for your work comes when you do not know what you really want. The absence of a clear personal mission and not having a well-defined goal in harmony with your inner self is the root cause of the problem. You and your inner self are not clear about what you want and how you are going to achieve it. What do you do in a situation like this? You simply do not do the work, and postponing is the best way to do just that. And I must admit to you here that in the days I just mentioned, I never really had a well-defined goal for my writings. But I was not consciously aware of it myself. I wanted to do more serious work but was not sure of what I wanted to do. I was not confident of myself and as a result I did not respect my work or myself enough to be able to adhere to my schedule. And this was the problem.

But now that I am focused, I know exactly what I want. I respect my work enough to be able to adhere to any schedule however difficult it may seem to be. I have become disciplined, and it has brought its own rewards.

When you get up at 4 in the morning for your assignment you have to respect your assignment enough to be able to leave the comfort of your bed so early in the morning; when you practise your music lesson while your friends are out in the fields playing you have to be focused on your music with the desire and the confidence to be able to excel in it in future; when you do not eat what is not good for you, you have to respect your future health enough; and when you do not buy what you think you cannot afford at this point of time you have to be committed to not going into debt. When you respect yourself and your goal, you will stay focused and disciplined. Discipline is the ability to make yourself do what you want to do, irrespective of the fact that you do not want to do it then. And when you *really* want to do something you will find nothing tempting enough to stop you from doing just that.

> *Real glory springs from the silent conquest*
> *of ourselves, without that the conqueror is*
> *only the first slave.* —Thomson.

All meaningful things in life are done by people who do things on their own. Success of any significance is achieved when we work in areas that are not controlled by others. No one can force you to create anything new, to plan a new venture, to discover or invent something, to write a book, in short, to do anything that is not a routine. You have to be motivated from within, and to be able to sustain this motivation you have to be disciplined enough so as not to quit mid-way or stray from your goal. And discipline you know is being focused.

It is said that to like others you have to first like yourself. And to truly like your self (in the right way) you have to have mastery over yourself. Self-mastery promotes self-confidence, which in turn promotes self-discipline, which is the basis of true independence. Independence, courage and co-operation are essential to mature and balanced handling of every situation and in making it possible to pursue our goals with conviction. To be disciplined means overcoming our weaknesses and fears and working towards what we really want.

> *To rule self and subdue our passions is more praiseworthy because so few know how to do it.* —Guiccardini.

To be committed to our work does not mean we have to have rigid schedules or to ignore our responsibilities; it simply means to honour our schedules and our resolves along with our responsibilities, to have mastery over our desires and our wants that are not in harmony with our true selves, to know what is right for us and to be able to do what we ought to do so that we can achieve what we want to achieve. This does not mean we have to lose focus of our responsibilities, it simply means we should not use our responsibilities as excuses for losing the focus of our goals.

Studies have shown that children who learn the lesson of discipline early in life do better when they grow up. This is because a child who is self-disciplined has already learned to define his goals and to keep them in mind; his goals are also likely to be in harmony with his inner self and he does not need outside restrictions to keep him focused on them. And he carries this quality with him when he grows up.

To be able to honour your commitments you have to be committed to your commitments. Just keep these facts in mind.

1. You cannot achieve anything significant in life till you are committed to your work.
2. To be committed to your work you have to be disciplined.
3. To be disciplined you have to have your goals set in accordance with your values and be focused on them.
4. You should respect yourself and your work enough so as not to be distracted by other temptations.

Rule
Ten

Be a Victor; Not a Victim

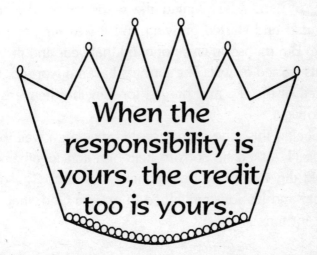

When the responsibility is yours, the credit too is yours.

Take charge of your Life
Do not let others, or circumstances, control you

The hand that holds the strings,
Controls the swing.

Responsibility educates.—Wendell Phillips.

Once there were two farmers. They had adjoining fields. When it was time to sow they tilled their land and planted the seeds. Soon the seeds sprouted and started growing and it was time to water them. But monsoon was not good that year and the little plants started to wilt. The farmers became worried, they looked at the sky and prayed for rain, but heavens did not oblige.

Seeing this, one farmer started digging a well to get water. He asked his sons to help him and together they would dig every day from sunrise to sunset. The other farmer and his sons continued to pray to God, they had faith in him.

Soon the first farmer hit water and his well filled up in time for him to save his plants. He had a bumper crop that year.

The other farmer's field dried, and he had to face drought.

The question here is, was the first farmer lucky or did he bring luck to himself? Can God help you if you do not help yourself?

Always remember, your life is your life, and you, and only you, are the chief player in it. You are the hero of your life and no one, absolutely no one, can displace you from your place.

> Philip C. McGraw says, *you are accountable for your life. Good or bad, successful or unsuccessful, happy or sad, fair or unfair, you own your life.*

If you are a grown up adult, leading an independent life, are financially self-sufficient, then let me tell you that whatever has happened to you in the past and whatever is happening to you today is the result of the choices you have made during the course of your life. It is the outcome of your personal reaction to the various situations you have come across, and every situation can be perceived differently you know. Everything good, bad, or indifferent, fortunate or unfortunate, your successes and failures, are the result of the choices you have made. You could have done this directly or indirectly, knowingly or unknowingly, but all that you have got today, or that has happened to you, or is happening to you is the result of the choices you have made and acted upon, or even not acted upon. When you choose not to act that also is a choice you made, and you are responsible for the outcome whatever it may be.

Now, you could be feeling outraged by my suggestion of your responsibility for the wrongs that have happened in your life and you could be wanting to say 'I am, in no way, going to take this suggestion of yours, I am definitely not accountable for all the mess in my life, after all I am a victim of my circumstances and my misfortunes, and you hold me responsible for all that was beyond my control. No, I can never accept this nonsense.'

To this, let me tell you dear reader, you are not the only one likely to feel this way, majority of the readers would. After all, it is human nature not to own responsibility for any mistake. No one wants to be blamed for the chaos in his life, but is keen to take the credit any way.

*Much misconstruction and bitterness are
spared to him who thinks naturally upon*

what he owes to others rather than what he
ought to expect from them.—Mad.Guizot.

I will like to point out to you here that accepting responsibility for your behaviour does not amount to blaming yourself; it is in fact the opposite of it. Accepting responsibility denotes having faith in yourself and your ability to learn and change, it is getting out of the negative mindset of a victim; it means becoming a victor instead.

Now I shall ask you to pause for a moment and reflect very carefully on what I have to say to you. Just relax and clear your mind of all prejudices you may have to any suggestion of accepting the responsibility for your life. Open your mind to new ways of looking at things. You know that if you want to change your future you will have to change your present; you will have to change your way of interpreting situations and reacting to them.

Now return to what you have just read about your role in your life.

Are you feeling assaulted by my suggestion of your accountability? If so, this reaction is *your choice*.

Are you feeling miserable that this may really be so? This again is *your choice*.

Are you feeling confident that if it is so you can improve your life and move ahead? This also is *your choice*.

Are you feeling happy and in control of your life? This is *your choice* too.

See how your different reactions to the same suggestion are your doing and will influence the outcome. In the first two situations your reaction is of a victim and it does not help anyone to play the victim, in the other two situations your reaction is of a victor where you are in control of the situation. As you have reacted differently to this single suggestion you perceive and react differently to every situation in your life too, and this influences what you get out of your life.

You may now say that you were mishandled as a child, were abused or neglected by those who were entrusted with your care, and it has left its scars on you. And this is what is coming in the way of your progress and you are unable to do what you really want to do. Abuse of children is a very tragic and unfortunate reality that does happen and children are victims without being in any way responsible for what happens to them. Children are always innocent, they are never accountable for the behaviour of the adults in their lives, and they can be victims of the worst kind of abuse that can definitely leave scars on them.

We do come across people who were unfortunate as children and now, as adults, are unable to cope with their lives. And if you are one of those unfortunate ones then it is indeed lamentable that it is so. But now that you are a grown up adult, in control of your thoughts and your life, you should try and figure out how you can best help yourself and come out of this abuse. It is important that you heal yourself. Self-healing is in your hands, it may be difficult, but it can still be done however difficult or complicated it may be. This I can assure you.

The past has happened and sealed itself, and your future is yet to take shape. Not to continue to be a victim of your past is in your hands now. I know it is easier said than done, but it can be done and that is what should matter to you now. This is your biggest hope. This in no way amounts to condoning the behaviour of the wrong doer, it is only a way to bring you out of the control he will continue to have on you as long as you are not able to heal yourself. You will continue being his victim till you forget him and move on. To be able to do this is the greatest power you have, use it. Fill the colours on the canvas of your future yourself. A little help from a person, especially trained for this can be of great help here. Leaving your unhappy past behind and marching ahead will give you the freedom and courage you need to transform yourself into a new person.

You may also, at times, feel like a victim of your circumstances, a difficult boss, non-cooperative spouse, irresponsible kids, lack of opportunities in your life, sudden death in the family that placed responsibilities on you, your bad health, sex, class and race, all could influence the choices that you are making, but as long as you have choices you have hope. You will find many successful people who had similar problems like you have but they were able to get over them, and you can too.

The problem with feeling a victim is that it provides a false sense of security; it absolves you of your part in your misfortune. You feel you are not the creator of the mess that your life is in, and this makes you feel good in a very negative way. But like every negative trait, it cannot bring positive results.

Recognising your accountability is crucial to your success. When you know how you influenced your past and how you can influence your future it gives you a sense of power and hope.

> *Responsibility walks hand in hand with capacity and power.* —J.G.Holland.

Taking this power in your hands is not as difficult as you may think. The best way to do it is to reflect on a situation from your past where you strongly feel you were a victim of your circumstances or the people around you, or both. Replay the whole event in your mind and see what happened and how it happened. See if there was anything you could have done differently to alter the situation or to prevent it. Or could you even have interpreted it differently so that it had a different impact on you? See if it was really as bad as it hurts, or is it that you are hurting more than you ought to? Negative reactions to any situation have a tendency to grow with the time; we feed them with resulting negative thoughts.

Do this exercise with every situation that is hurting you and is coming in your way to success. This is crucial in helping you to recognise your role in your life and to make you understand that it is *you*, and only you, who can change your destiny and achieve your goals whatever they may be. Blaming others may absolve you of your responsibility but it can achieve nothing except to frustrate you and make you bitter, and that is not what you are aiming at when you want to improve. And as you are holding this book in your hands it is evidence of your being serious about improving your life and emerging a victor. Recognising your mistakes may be painful for some time but it also brings hope along with it, and that is its greatest reward.

I know you could be finding it difficult to accept and to follow what I am telling you to do. After all it is so much easier to blame all the wrongs of your life on someone else, be it parents, teachers, friends, neighbours, associates, genes, luck and what not, than to take the accountability on yourself. It is human to look for and put the blame on others and the more we do it the more proficient we become, and the more distant we move from our goal too.

Researchers are trying to find answer to every problem in our genes; they are also there looking for every solution in our behaviour. Some will tell us how our medical problems are also of our making, others will tell us how we inherit criminal tendencies as well. It is up to us to listen to whom so ever we like. This too is our choice. Just keep this in mind, when you blame others, you may feel good for some time but you do not have hope and you don't improve, when you blame yourself, you may feel bad for some time but you have hope and you improve.

> *On its highest level man's contemporary desire to escape responsibility expresses itself not in emphasis on luck, or emotional submission to fate, but in a thorough going deterministic theory, ascribing all personal qualities to heredity and environment.*
> —Harry Emerson Fosdick.

However much you may like it or even enjoy it, playing the victim cannot take you anywhere. It will be negative satisfaction, and negative satisfactions are always marked with frustration and resentment, never success. Taking accountability on the other hand will open the doors to improvement and build your self-confidence. This is the only way to change what you want to change, the way you want to change when you want to change. This will lead you to your road to success dwarfing your problems on the way.

Accepting accountability of your life is crucial to your success. Keep these points in mind and march on your road to success.

1. Always know that your life is your life and no one else is accountable for it.
2. Never play the victim; it never helps.
3. Even if you were a victim as a child try to come out of your past and move ahead. This is the only way to get out of the evil grip that could be holding you back.
4. Analyse your past situations and see how you could be responsible for what happened and how you can change for the future.
5. It is up to you to understand your role in your life and work on it. When you have your life in your control, you can march to success.